Inside A Rainforest
Royal Court

Fidelia Nimmons

Contributors:

Hon Barrister Patrick Aigbogun
Bernadette Aigbogun
Chief Sunday Aigbogun (Late) Chief Ebenzer of Igueben

Preface

Great Kingdom of Benin was probably the greatest Kingdom to exist in West Africa. Things changed with European colonisation of Africa in the 19th century. Its story however continues to intrigue and excite scholars and historians alike.

The kingdom's people hold fast to their ancestral customs, adapting when they need to e.g. in embracing Christianity and modern influences from other countries and cultures particularly the West.

How to use:
You will find a glossary at the end of the book which explains specialist words written in red throughout the book.

Words in the glossary are grouped according to the section where they are used.

Some brain teaser questions have been included at the back for those interested in a bit of challenge.

A list of websites for further reading is included at the back under bibliography.

Volume 2 of this book *Inside A Rainforest Court: Growing up* presents information on aspects of life like Childhood and marriage.

Contents

Location

Below is location of Great Kingdom of Benin before colonisation in Africa.

The modern kingdom is located in modern day Nigeria in West Africa.

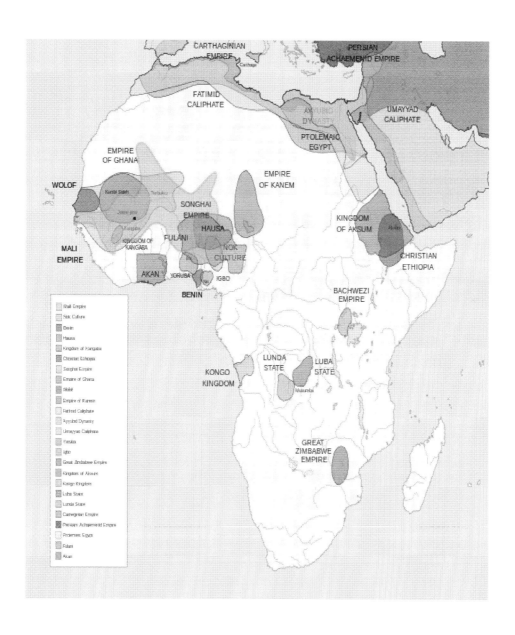

Background information:

The Kingdom of Benin was one of the Forest Kingdoms of ancient Africa. It was founded by the Edo or Bini people during the 14th century, reached its height with a powerful Royal court in the 15th century, before it was finally conquered in the 19th century.

The Kingdom of Benin was not located in the modern country of Benin, but was instead part of what is now southern Nigeria. There are therefore two Benin's: one is the ancient kingdom and the other is a modern country in Africa, which is not part of modern day Nigeria.

The culture of Benin has changed little since ancient times and traditions such as their royal family, chieftaincy, art, and oral folklore continue to thrive to this day as a way of preserving the Benin customs.

History timelines

World History Timeline

2686 - 525 BC
Ancient Egypt

40BC
Ubini (Benin) Kingdom founded

750 - 30 BC
Ancient Greece

146 BC - 400 AD
Ancient Rome

410 - 1065
Invaders

900- 1100
Ogiso Kings rule Benin

1200
Oba Eweka begins
the Oba era in Benin

1216 - 1347
Middle Ages

1485 - 1602
Tudors

1819 - 1901
Victorians

1897
End of Ancient Benin

1914
Modern Benin

Kings of Benin timeline

EARLY PERIOD

Early 14th century
or before

c. late 14th century

c. early 15th century

WARRIOR KINGS
c. mid- 15th century

c. late 15th century
to early 16th century

Late 16th century
CRISIS AND RENEWAL

c. late 17th century

c. 1715
c. 1735
c.1750
c.1804

c.1815
c. 1850
END OF THE KINGDOM
NEW PERIOD
1933
1979

Ogiso kings
Oranmiyan
1. Eweka 1
2. Uwakhuahen
3. Ehenmihen
4. Ewedo
5. Oguola
6. Edoni
7. Udagbedo
8. Ohen
9. Egbeka
10. Orobiru
11. Uwaifiokun
12. Ewuare
13. Ezoti
14. Olua
15. Ozolua
16. Esigie
17. Orhoghua
18. Ehengbuda
19. Ohuan
20. Ohenzae
21. Akenzae
22. Akengboi
23. Akenkpaye
24. Akengbedo
25. Ore-oghenen
26. Ewuakpe
27. Ozuere
28 Akenzua
29. Eresoyen
30. Akengbuda
31. Obanosa
32. Ogbebo
33. Osemwede
34. Adolo
35. Ovoranmwen
36. Eweka 11
37. Akenzua 11
38. Erediauwa

A Bini creation story.

In the beginning, there were no land only waters.

At the centre of the waters stood a tree and on its top lived Owonwon, the toucan.

When Osanobua decided to populate the world, he gathered his three sons and sent them off in a canoe. Each was given the choice of one gift to take with him.

The two elder sons chose wealth and craft tools. As the youngest prepared to choose his own gift, Owonwon cried out to him to take a snail shell. This he did, and when the canoe reached the centre of the waters the youngest son turned the shell upside down and out poured an endless stream of sand. In this manner, the land began to emerge from the waters. The sons of Osanobua were afraid to go out of the canoe and so the chameleon was sent to test the firmness of the ground. From that time on, it walks with a hesitating step.

The place where the land emerged was called Agbon, "the world", at Agbon, Osanobua first came down from the sky on a chain and demarcated the world. It was from there that he sent people to the four corners of the earth, to every country and geographic realm. He made his youngest son the ruler of Benin, the owner of the land and he established his own realm, the spirit world, across the waters where the sky and earth meet.

So began the story of a kingdom that was to become great in time, a kingdom where the gods intermingled with people and their affairs on a daily basis; a kingdom where the people had to keep the gods happy to keep them on side; a kingdom whose king was a son of the chief god Osanobua; a king who had intimate relationships with the gods; a king with powers to intervene in the gods' decisions regarding the people and most important of all, a king who could switch easily between the tangible world and the spiritual realm.

Government
The Oba

The Oba - *the divine kingship.* **The Edo** believed that the Oba was divine, this was reflected in their day to day way of life and extended to all areas including political, religious and social aspects. Bini oral traditions, has it that the Oba descended from Oranmiyan, a Yoruba Prince from Ife whom they had invited to be their king when they became dissatisfied with their previous one. The Oba ruled on the virtue of this alone.

The Oba's political powers were extensive, he was the last resort in court matters and he alone could issue the death penalty. He owned all the land in the kingdom and all taxes and tributes were paid to him. He also controlled external trade. His army was well trained and the best during that time.

Benin Bronzes showing a Portuguese soldier with musket. The Portuguese trained the Benin army and fought alongside them in many wars.

Court life

The Oba lived in a vast area of land to accommodate, residential areas for his numerous wives and small children, meeting chambers for various groups of chiefs, storehouses, shrines and alters and work areas for ritual specialists and royal craftsmen. In short the palace was a busy place; with hustling and bustling noises of activities carried out by the multitudes of officials, servants, family members and chiefs.

Early Dutch travellers described the royal palace as divided into many magnificent palaces, houses and apartments, and comprises beautiful and long square galleries, about as long as the Exchange at Amsterdam. The palace was said to be as large as the town of Haarlem.

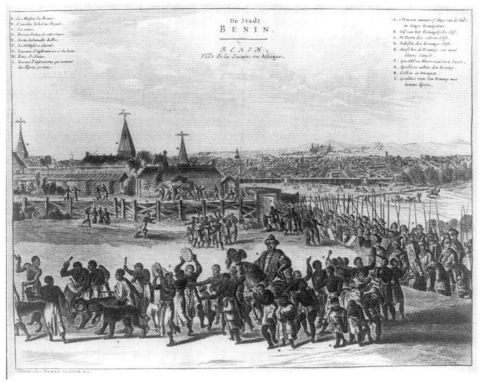

View of Benin City with Oba in procession engraved in early 17th century by Olfert Dapper (1668).

He described 'The Oba shews himself only once a year to his people, going out of his court on horseback, beautifully attired with all sorts of royal ornaments, and accompanied by three to four hundred noblemen on horseback and on foot, and a great number of musicians before and behind him, playing merry tunes on all sorts of instruments'.

The Oba on horse back

In Edo custom, only the Oba was allowed to ride side-saddle on his horse.
Here two attendants use their shields to shade him from the elements.

What jobs do you think the pages did in the palace?

Administration

The Ancient Chiefs
The titled chiefs together with the royal family made up the political elites of the kingdom.

Chieftaincy pecking order
There three chiftancy groups with specialised dutietes. These were:

1) The Seven Uzama –
These were considered the descendants of the very elders of Benin who had sent to Ife for Oranmiyan.
They were the 'guardians of Benin custom'.
They installed new kings.
They took active roles in the annual worship of the departed ones.

2) The Palace Chiefs -
They lived in ogbe- the king's sector of the city.
They were members of well established urban families.
They were concerned with the administration of the palace.

They belonged to one of the three important palace associations:

Iwebo
- Cared for the Oba's regalia
- Supervised the craftsmen
- Conducted negotiations with European traders visiting Benin.

Ibiwe
- Cared for the oba's wives and children

Iweguae
- They provided the Oba's domestic staff of officials, cooks, servants and pages.

3) The Town Chiefs -

They rose to position by own efforts not by inherited wealth or connections.

They were responsible for running the various territory of the kingdom.

They collected taxes for the Oba.

They conscripted soldiers.

They mediated between village and royal interests.

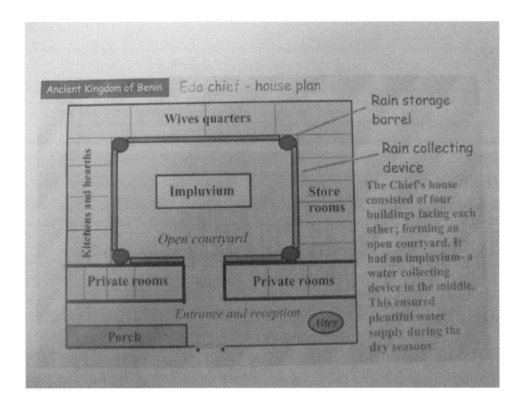

Activity: Imagine that you were one of the Oba's chiefs; make a diary entry of a day in your life.

Modern day Chief Swearing-in Ceremony in pictures

The court officials assemble for the ceremony to begin. Can you see the priestess in red? What do you think her duties are?

Notice the chief's wives hairstyles.

The whole community gathers. The musicians are in place ready to make music. (1996).

The ceremony begins.

The Enogie (local Oba) arrives for the ceremony. Notice his regalia.

The Chiefs wives are cleansed as part of the ceremony. Notice the purified white chalk marks.

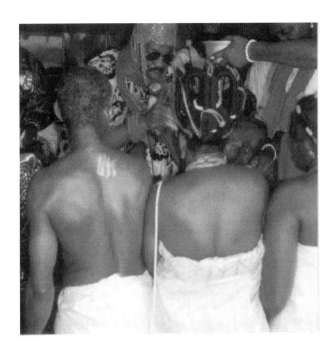

First the wives swear an oath of support for the chief's position.

The chief then swears an oath and receives his ceremonial necklace.

Next he receives his ceremonial crown.

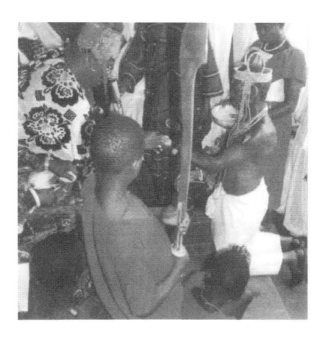

The Enogie cleanses the chief .

Finally the chief receives his sword of office.

Ceremonial Emblems

Eben - is the official symbol of authority handed over to the chief by the king.

Ada - the symbol of the higher authority possessed by the king. He alone has the authority to execute a capital offender.

Enogie of Igueben in sitting (the Ada Bearer in front of him).

The Ebenze of Igueben goes on a walkabout, the drummers in the background, still making music.

Conferment of chieftaincy title now complete, it is time for community celebration.

Chief sits with his Eben in front of him. This is his emblem of authority. Chief is now part of the council that meet regularly with the Enogie and sometimes with the Oba's council to discuss issues that affect the people and ongoing preservation of Edo culture.

Early 19th century Oba of Benin

Current Oba of Benin

Death and Burial

Just like the Egyptians, Edos believed in *Afterlife:* that the soul rejoined the body after burial.

When an Oba died, he was buried in his full royal regalia and with an entourage to help establish his new kingdom and to take care of his every need. Believed to be essential were a band of slaves to serve him and a wife to cook for him. The slaves were buried first, then the wife and finally the Oba placed on top them to show his importance and authority.

Succession

The first born son of the Oba was always the heir and since he was allowed many wives, several sons were produced, this caused rivalry and made it difficult to tell who was really first born. To get round this problem, potential rivals were sent to the countryside as hereditary rulers (Enogie) over administrative districts.

An elaborate ceremony described below follows interment; the same order was and is still observed for the king as his chiefs.

A royal Chief burial ceremony

The Edos in history have always had elaborate rituals to ensure smooth transition of the deceased between the tangible world and the spiritual realm. The Chiefs and elders who are the principal custodians of Edo customs and traditions defend these practices rigorously particularly in relation to the Royal families. The only change over time is a full court is no longer buried with the King.

When a chief dies, this is kept secret until all the village chiefs, elders and his first born son have been informed and gathered. They then carry out secret rituals behind closed doors and agree course of events over the coming days and months.

Cannon shots are used to announce the passing away of the chief.

From now on, the elders hold planning meetings regularly on the burial ceremony procedures. The wives go into mourning. They wear black clothes and cannot attend public gatherings like market or parties for three months. They are allocated companions for this period.

When initial ceremonies have been completed cannon shots are fired again to announce commencement of chief's interment and again at the end.

The shots fired must be in odd numbers 3, 5, 7, 9, 11. Same number of shots is fired each time in a particular ceremony. The village Chiefs, elders and first born sons must decide this at the initial planning stages.

The traditional burial ceremony can last from one to five days. In the past it lasted seven days.

During the course of the celebration, the family feed the whole community who join in various activities during the day. Each day, this involves slaughtering some cows and goats and cooking cauldrons of rice and pounded yam are cooked. Crates of drinks which must not run out during the ceremony are also supplied.

Day 1:

Early morning on Day 1 Cannon shots wake the people up to announce the beginning of the ceremonies.

Today, there is an all night celebration of Chief's life. The community join with the children to eat, drink and dance all night long.

The wives do not join in the celebration as they are in mourning.

Cannon shots

11 cannon shots are fired each time there is change of events and activities or someone important arrives.

The number of cannon shots has to be odd number, i.e. 3, 5, 7, 9 or 11.

The family decides how many will be fired each day during the course of the ceremony and this depends on their funds.

After the cannon shots, the Chiefs and village elders begin to gather for the day's events and ceremony.

They are in charge of the ceremonies and work hand in hand with the sons and family members on the procedures and rituals.

Punctuality is essential as the ceremonies cannot begin until every chief and elder has arrived.

The drinks must be kept flowing, the host must keep filling the crates and keep up with the kola nuts supply.

The village women elders sit away from the men. They have no say in the procedures.

Days 2 and 3

Various celebration events like masquerades entertaining the community; lots of feasting takes place with the community singing and dancing. General merriment is the order of the day.

In ancient practice, a bronze horn blower was part of the music band to entertain.

Day 4

All the married daughters are expected to come back from whichever part of the world they live in; to ensure their father gives them that final blessing before he proceeds to the spirit world. They bring various gifts to the elders to intercede on their behalf to ensure that this happens. The elders receive the gifts and pray for them.

A moderator is appointed and all negotiations are done through him. Items value could be translated into monetary terms, if this is more convenient.

The chiefs agree a levy based on factors like how often this child visits home and their past contributions to the family. The less prominent the child has been, the higher the levy. The Moderator must step in to challenge all excessive levies; he must on behalf of each daughter, put the first offer on the table. The chiefs can reject this until an acceptable offer is reached.

List of levy items
- Kola nuts
- Kegs of palm wine
- Kegs of palm kernal
- A bale of traditional African fabric
- Goats
- A bundle of yams
- Money (could be exuberant)

Day 5

Today is the last day of the ceremonies; the deceased properties will be shared out to only 1st born male offsprings

Cannon shots wake people up.

- ✓ The chiefs and village elders gather
- ✓ Masquerades entertain the guests
- ✓ All other rituals are completed today
- ✓ Food and drinks are still flowing.

The issue for the assembly is whether the deceased owed anyone, after that the sons are allocated their inheritance. They could share this with others at a later date.

Each son slaughters a cow which the elders share among themselves; this being the last tribute.

The chiefs and elders have made a lot of money from their own shares of the various levies they have imposed on the children and family.

The burial ceremonies not only celebrate the chief's life, it also provides for a continuity of Edo traditions passed on in every fine point from generation to generation. As custodians of Edo cultures and traditions, during the ceremonies, the elders have:

- been accorded respect
- earned some income from the ceremonies
- received gifts during the period
- topped up on their food supply
- safeguarded the customs

Trade and Commerce

The Edos were very skilled carvers and blacksmiths, some of their bronze and terra cotta sculptures survive in very good state to this day.

They had extensive trade links and were known to be shrewd traders. Their style was one of rigorous negotiations and would only agree to a deal on their own terms. This meant that occasionally they negotiated for days, weeks or even months before sealing an agreement. It was therefore not an easy task to trade with them but there was always lots of profits to be made when this was successful.

The Edo traded with neighbouring nations as well as with other African Kingdoms who came from South, East and North Africa on horsebacks or by long treks. Crops traded included local produce like yams, beans, rice, gourds, cattle, sheep, goats, poultry, cotton, peanuts, sweet potatoes, cassava, vegetables and various fruit like paupua, mango, tangerines, oranges, coconut, bananas, plantain, and maize. They were also good suppliers of rubber from the rainforest.

On sea, the Edo traded with the Dutch and the Portuguese traders. Jewellery was a popular trade item. The Edos specialised in woven striped garments that were popular on the Gold Coast, blue fabric, pepper, jasper stones, and leopard skins. In exchange, they received Coral beads, red and silver fabrics - cotton, red velvet, embroidered silk, coarse flannel - candied oranges and lemons, mirrors, and iron bars.

The Edos did not use coins as money but cowrie shells which was introduced from East Africa in local trading and bronze manillas for trading with the Europeans. These are sometimes referred to as bronze bracelet money.

Cowrie shells were used as trading currency with local people.

Ivory Salt cellar. 'Afro-Portuguese ivories'.

Religion

The people of Benin just like in Greek mythology believed in many gods and goddesses.

They viewed the world at two levels, the spirit world and the human world and to them there was no clear boundaries between these. Also as in Greek mythology, the gods and spirits daily intervene in the lives of humans, powerful humans are said to draw upon the forces of the spirit world to give them supernatural powers to transform their daily experience (supernatural beings).

The Edos also held strong beliefs in spirits, magic, and the power of witch doctors.

The Oba was believed to have mystical powers.

The Oba's motif represents him with mudfish legs.
The motif represented the people's belief in the Oba's spiritual power to be able to bridge the physical tangible world realm to the

33

spiritual world of the gods. For just like the mudfish that can live on both water and land, the king can switch easily between the physical world realm and the gods' spiritual realm.

The gods hierarchy:

Osanobua - is the creator god, the high god who lives in magnificent palace, surrounded by courtiers and served by other deities. He is the father of other gods and assigns responsibilities of care for aspects of the world to them. He deals mainly with the spirit world and does not interfere with the running of the tangible world. He is appealed to only as a last resort, when all else has failed. He is utterly benevolent.

Olokun - is the first born son of Osanobua.
Responsibilities include the great oceans of the earth which surround the land and into which all the rivers flow. He is the provider of children to the Edo people, in particular beautiful women; he is therefore the god of beauty. He is the source of riches and good fortune. Exceptionally beautiful women are said to have been sent to earth by Olokun as his special devotees they kept a shrine and were priestess' to him.

Olokun's symbolic colour is white to show that he is a 'cool' god who, like his father represents the positive aspects of experiences: ritual purity, good luck, health, long life, prosperity and happiness.

Ogiuwu: Osanobua's other son is the god of the underworld, said to be bringer of death. He sends his messenger **Ofoe** (who is represented in Bini art as having only legs and arms) to earth to take human life. He chases his victims with his legs and catches them with his arms for return to Ogiuwu. Being a bad guy he is no longer prominent in Benin religious worship.

Ogiuwu's symbolic colour is black.

Ogun is Osanobua's junior son is patron of farmers, craftsmen, hunters, and warriors (all those who depend on tools). He was sent to the world to make farm and to make war. Ogun's devotees are protected by him and he uses his sword to open the way to a better life for them. They are thus progressive people.

The ceremonial swords the *eben and the ada* represent Ogun's powers as metallic objects of indestructibility. The Oba is said to be indestructible.

Ogun's symbolic colour is red which depicts sudden and violent actions, e.g. thunderstorm, fire, blood.

Osun- is god of the rainforest. He is said to reside in the leaves and herbs of the forest. Like his brother Ogun, he is concerned with how raw materials from the forest are processed and transformed into instruments of power which preserve and maintain life on earth.

His symbolic colour is red.

Religious festivals

The Edos celebrated lots of annual festivals in honour of their various gods and goddesses. The Oba led these ceremonies and wore ceremonial robes during these periods. He always carried a sword *the eben*, which was a symbol of his authority. There were many festivals including new yam harvest festivals to honour the gods, Ogun and Osun. All subjects had to stop work for several days to attend a festival. An example is the new yam festival which lasted for seven days and involved feasting and merry making for the whole period.

The Edos believed in work hard and play hard to achieve a healthy lifestyle.

Art

The Oba wanted people to see him as divine and powerful and went to great length to achieve this through art. He adorned his palace with hundreds of extravagant metal plaques produced by palace blacksmiths and carvers.

This resulted in Edo becoming famous for its sculpture and art, which were exported to other parts of the world through trade and to this day remain so.

The Oba had the sole control of the brass plaque production in the Kingdom. The Edo produced brass plaques for him only and if they broke this rule, they could be put to death.

Brass was chosen as a material for plaque making because it is metal and hard and long lasting just like the Oba. It showed the power of the Oba as indestructible and everlasting.

The plaques were generally small about 46 centimetres or one and a half feet tall. They were used to record Edo's achievements.

Carved wooden door at the palace show the ada and eben
and the Oba and attendants

Bronze plague showing the Oba of Benin with his attendants.
Notice the young pages. They spend years learning their jobs at the palace, today, attendants and receive a qualification and certificate certifying their position at the palace.

Queen Idia. Queen mother of Oba Esigie.

Bronze figure of a huntsman carrying an antelope with a dog at his knee. The bronze figures tell us about Edo's way of life, we can see from above that hunters used dogs to help them in hunt in the forest.

The King's Festival

The King's festival known as Igue festival is celebrated between Christmas and New Year. It has been celebrated since the time of Oba Ewuare, one of the warrior kings who reigned in the 15th century. During the festival, the king's divinity and magical powers were renewed and he blessed his people. Foreigners and non-natives were not allowed to see the king during the festival period. It was also a great time of feasting for the people.

Here its celebration is presented in the form of palace news:

This Year's Igue Festival

Here are some things you need to remember throughout the 9 days festival:

1. The reason you have not seen His Majesty and some of his chiefs for some days now is that they have been preparing for the Igue festival by completing the Agwe (fasting). So when you see them for the first time on the first day, you need to cheer at the top of your vocal cords. Your cheerful noise will encourage and reassure them that they have your full support as a people.

2. Remember that unless you are a chief, you must arrive early each day to get a good spot to watch the celebration from; otherwise you will not be able to see a thing. Try to get out of bed as soon as the cock crows, have a proper bath, adorn yourself in your finest attire and jewellery, have a good meal and head straight for the palace to secure your space.

3. If you are accompanying a chief as part of his entourage, remember to get his own programme the day before otherwise, you will find that you have been pushed out of your role and limelight; it is after all a great honour to be accompanying a chief to these celebrations.

4. Remember to be on your best behaviour, no offhand comment and cheer as loudly as you can for every single activity by the Oba

or his chiefs. You are there to show your support for His Majesty and his great Chiefs, so do so very enthusiastically.

5. Have a good rest each night so you are refreshed for the next day's activities and events.

6. Make sure that you manage to visit all chiefs' and other people's houses for some feasting and dancing and take care to make your presence felt, lavishing praises on their wives and children when they take the dance floor will not go unnoticed. You might be invited to join one of the youth clubs after this.

7. Remember that the festival is a time for observing our religious rituals as well as a time for merry making, feasting, wining, dining and dancing. It is very important to enjoy yourself.

8. Plan how you will use the nine days fruitfully to gain the most from all the generosity people will be showing. This means make the most of it or you could miss out on a freebee. The Chiefs normally give out souvenirs like wooden Ise game boards carved in their images on it; you could also collect some free spending money they give out as tips or when you get 'showered' during your dance. Be creative and use your full imagination during the nine days!

Programme of Events

Day 1: His Majesty dresses in his ceremonial robes and sits on the royal throne. His High ranking chiefs led by the Iyase (the Prime Minister) pay homage to him by dancing with their Eben emblem. The Ubi ritual of wading off evil spirits takes place. The Oba blesses all the homes in the kingdom through the Ewere. The Oba and his chiefs pay homage at our ancestral shrines.

Day 2: Ritual day. The Efas (the blessings priests) sanctify His Majesty with white chalk on his forehead . His Majesty blesses the sacrificial items. The high priest the Isekhure cleanses and slaughters the animals in a special ritual. His Majesty, his chiefs and members of the palace societies are anointed.

Day 3: Members of the Royal family, the Princes and Princesses dance to honour His Majesty and the kingdom.

Day 4: Free day for community celebrations and activities like masquerades, Feasting, dining and lots of dancing. Groups of friends and family members visit each other's houses to enjoy the feast each household has prepared. Spend all day in merriment, feasting and dancing.

Day 5: Free day for community celebrations and activities like masquerades, Feasting, dining and lots of dancing. Groups of friends and family members visit each other's houses to enjoy the feast each household has prepared. Spend all day in merriment, feasting and dancing. Visit the houses you haven't yet.

Day 6: Edo people – the whole community celebrate and visit and dance for the Oba to honour him.

Day 7: Free day for community celebrations and activities like masquerades, Feasting, dining and lots of dancing. Groups of friends and family members visit each other's houses to enjoy the feast each household has prepared. Spend all day in merriment, feasting and dancing. Visit the houses you haven't yet.

Day 8: Free day for community celebrations and activities like masquerades, Feasting, dining and lots of dancing. Groups of friends and family members visit each other's houses to enjoy the feast each household has prepared. Spend all day in merriment, feasting and dancing. Visit the houses you haven't yet.

Day 9: Last day of celebration, by now you should have visited all houses and joined in their celebration and feasting. Remember no one should be left out, check that you have seen everyone, we are one unit this festival time; we eat from the same pot and drink from the same keg. The Enogies (Outskirts rulers) must now set their own dates for celebrating their festival in the same fashion back in their domain. These will be around the New Year.

Remember that there should be no burial ceremony taking place during the festival period.

Please ensure that you have prepared well in advance for the events.

Have fun!

It was and still is a great time of feasting and celebration for the community.

Slavery

The Edos acquired slaves for debt recovery purposes or insolvency, avenging maltreatment or captured in war. In some cases slaves were born into slavery. The Edos did not engage in buying and selling of slaves like other Kingdoms and nations. Maltreating a slave was not part of the Edo culture.

The slave children had the same experiences as the household children except that if a slave child had something the other child wanted, s/he had to give it up and in some households had to be served food last. Slave children did most of the work the other children refused to do. They joined in games and other activities when they were not working.

Slave girls after a long service sometimes became one of the many wives of house master. Slave boys who worked out their time gained their freedom; they could also marry into the household and become family members enjoying privileges of the family.

This meant that slaves could buy their freedom by paying their master the price of their purpose or by marrying into the household.

Food

Most Edo people were farmers and grew their own food. Children were taught to farm from a very early age. As people were busy farming or doing other jobs during the day, the Edo meal consisted of one large meal in the evening. Here is a typical Edo daily meal:

Breakfast:
- Roasted plantain or corn with fruit

Lunch:
- Light meal e.g. cassava garri with meat or fish with friut
- Roasted yam or plantain with palm oil and fruit

Dinner:
- Feast of Pounded yam or yam and cassava (fou-Fou) fill up with eba (cassava paste).
- Vegetable soup with fresh and dry meat, bushmeat, snails, crayfish and fresh or dry fish.
- More fruit and vegetables; washed down with spring water and palm wine for the men.

Young children preferred the sweet plantain or sweet potato and fruit to pounded yam.

Rice meal was a treat or reserved for celebration days.

Festive food:
During festive seasons, the Edo sent food gifts to friends, family and the nobles. This included game meat, goats, chickens, fish, bundles of yams and kegs of palm wine and occasionally bundles of corn head. The generosity of the sender depended on how wealthy he was, in this case how fruitful his harvest has been, therefore the more food gifts they gave out, the more highly they were regarded by others.

During these festive days, known as Ukpe, Edos woke up at the crack of dawn to prepare cauldrons of food. Part of this they sent to neighbours, families and friends as token of good wishes, the remaining was served throughout the day to visitors, who came in mainly to wine and dine. Everyone went into each other's house and ate as much as they wanted as the whole community becomes one. During the day, all households maintained an open door policy and were not expected to run out of food.

This cooking, wining and dining as a single community unit continued for the five days of celebration.

Festive food list:

Kola nuts

- Yam - Boiled or pounded
- Cassava: as garri or mixed with pounded yam.
- Cocoyam pounded with yam, when this is in short supply
- Corn and Maize Roasted of ground
- Dried beans for making akara, mai-mai, etc
- Vegetables for soup making e.g. Egusi (melon seeds), ogbono, okra, spinach, water leaf, bitter leaf, nut meg, pepper,
- Fruit e.g. Mango, paw-paw, oranges, tangerines, cashew, guava, forest berries
- Meat- bush meat, antelopes, boars, pork, chicken, cows. goats, sheep,
- Fish- Fresh and dried or smoked.
- Drinks - Palm wine, coconut drink, local gin, spring water.

Rich households had more visitors than others and had to provide more food than others. Some used up to ten cows, twenty four goats, fifty chickens and countless games for cooking during the festive season (five days).

Activity: Try out a couple of the recipes in the resources section. Remember Edos did not use knives and forks to eat. You must use your fingers.

End of Old Kingdom
The end of an era

The kingdom of Benin began to decline with events elsewhere especially in Europe. It was hastened with the coming of the British who were out to expand their protectorates in Africa. They saw Edos as a hindrance to their advancement into the interiors of Africa and when a dispute broke out about the signing over of the kingdom to the British, they were quick to send in a punitive expedition, which burnt down and looted the royal palace and major buildings in Benin City thus ending the era of a powerful and progressive Rainforest Kingdom.

Sequence of events

Who was involved in The Benin Massacre of 1897:

1892 Oba Ovonramwen - tricked into signing protectorate treaty by Henry Gallwey.

Dispute breaks out about terms and intents of the treaty. Oba Ovonramwen bars all British officials and traders from entering Benin territories.

March 1896 - Oba Ovonramwen closes all trade routes along the coast, puts a trade embargo in place. The British are unhappy.

December 1896 - Consul Philips - violates Edo's custom. Insists and enters the Kingdom during an important religious festival for sons of the land only (the five-day Igue festival). This despite repeated advice from the king to wait till after the festival.

Chief Ologboshere and other chiefs - demand atonement to appease the gods.

Chief Ologboshere and selected soldiers from the Edo skilled army force are sent to the border at Gwato to stop Consul Philip entering the kingdom and disturbing the festival.

There is a dispute about what happened next but on:

4th January 1897 - four white men including Captain Philips and his 250 African attendants are killed as they forcefully try to enter the kingdom. Two White men escape by hiding in the forest.

January 12 1897 - the British form the Benin Punitive expedition to capture the king and destroy Benin City.

February 9 1897 - The British declare war. Benin soldiers defend their city fiercely and pluckily, a British battalion is routed and its commander beheaded. The war continues for ten days.

19th February - British troupes seize Benin

Between 19th and 21st February - British troupes shell Benin City setting it ablaze. They march through the city with firearms, shooting everything in sight. They burn down and loot the palace and senior chiefs' houses; they kill some high ranking chiefs.

With their city burnt down, the Edo people flee into neighbouring villages.

August 1897 - Oba Ovonramwen surrenders.

September 1897 - Queen Victoria's chief agent, Consul-General Ralph Moore tries Oba Ovonramwen and his remaining chiefs. He sentences Chief Ologboshere and three other chiefs to death. They are hanged.

Oba Ovonramwen is exiled to Calabar.

Without a ruler, Edo people lose their will and surrender to British rule.

Late 1897 - looted artworks from Benin are auctioned in Paris, France. They eventually, end up in private collections and museums across the world.

Oba Ovonramwen dies in 1914 whilst on exile in Calabar.

The British restore the crown returning ceased royal regalia.

Prince Aiguobasimwin is crowned as **Oba Eweka 11**.

Oba Eweka 11 rebuilds the palace in its current site though on a much smaller scale than the old palace.

A new era begins for the Edo people.

Oba Ovonramwen (1888 – 1914) last king of the old kingdom

Modern Benin

King Eweka 11, the Lion-heart was a very well educated king who used his diplomatic skills to persuade the British to restore the Benin monarchy. His argument was that the Edo monarchy was on par with the British and once his request was granted, he set about rebuilding the royal palace. He was also a very skilled and accomplished carver and blacksmith. Using these skills he built the palace which is occupied by the present Oba of Benin.

The Benin traditional institution has since changed in a number of ways including:

The Elected governor of Edo state must approve any crowned royal before he is given the official staff of office.

The Elected governor of Edo state has the power to remove a king.

Submission to a monarch's jurisdiction is optional although the local people rarely go against it.

The Courts have the overall say in jurisdiction matters.

The District Enogies and Chiefs have also had to adapt to changing times e.g. after being crowned traditionally, they still seek the recognition of the elected governor and in judicial matters submit to the courts.

The Oba of Benin in sitting. Make a sketch drawing of one of the personal attendants.

His Majesty Erediauwa 1

Oba of Benin

Omo'N'Oba

The supreme ruler of the Edo people

Current king of Benin Kingdom

Statues in Benin City

House of Assembly meeting

Oba Akenzua 11 2nd King in new Era

Edo warrior

Glossary

Benin Background page

Ancient - a long time ago

Chieftaincy - high ranking official

Customs - people's way of life

Divine - being or having the nature of a god

Forest Kingdom - a forest area that were ruled by a local king

Heir - successor: a person who inherits some title or office

Oral traditions - passed down from generation to generation by word of mouth.

Shrine - An altar or niche dedicated to a particular Goddess or God and held to be sacred.

Virtue - the quality of doing what is right and avoiding what is wrong

Modern Chief Swearing in ceremony page

Conferment - bestowal: the act of conferring an honour

Descendants - Ones Children, Grandchildren, Great-grandchildren, etc.

Mediated - acting or brought about through an intervening agency

Official - a worker who holds or is invested with an office

Political elite - A small group of people with a disproportionate amount of public decision-making power.

Terra cotta - Fired clay (literally 'baked earth')

Childhood page

Commerce - trade or exchange of goods and money.

Crop preservation - the activity of protecting the yield from plants in a single growing season from loss or danger

Drought - a prolonged period of dryness that can cause damage to plants.

Games - animals hunted for food or sport.

Produce - fresh fruits and vegetable grown for the market.

Trade and Commerce page

Blacksmith - A crafter of iron and steel.

Coral beads - Beads made from the hard stony skeleton of a Mediterranean coral that has a delicate red or pink colour

Cowrie shells - marine snails of the genus Cypraea (family Cypraeidae), found chiefly in tropical regions, especially around the Maldives or the East Indies. The shell itself is smooth and more or less egg-shaped, with a long, narrow, slit-like opening (aperture).

Dialects - a particular version of a language with its own distinctive accent, grammar and vocabulary.

Rural - sparsely settled places away from the influence of large cities and towns

Suitor - a man who courts a woman

Slavery page

Acquire - get: come into the possession of something concrete or abstract.

Insolvency - The inability of an individual or entity to pay its debts when they are due.

Maltreat - mistreat: treat badly.

Slave - a person who is owned by someone.

Privilege - a special advantage or immunity or benefit not enjoyed by all.

Religion page

Alter - a special surface or place set aside for magical workings and/or religious acknowledgement

Benevolent - generous in providing aid to others

Deities - or gods held in high regard and worshipped by human beings

Devotees - people who worship the god regularly

Mythology - Old stories that usually explain how something came to be

Priestess - woman who takes an officiating role in worship of any religion

Supernatural - Something that cannot be given an ordinary explanation

Art page

Brass - A yellowish alloy consisting mainly of copper and zinc

Ceremonies - a set of activities, infused with ritual significance and performed on certain occasions

Festivals - a set of celebrations in the honour of a god

Patron - someone who supports or favours some person, group, or institution

Underworld - in Classical mythology, this is the land of shadows where souls of the dead have to pass through to get to heaven or hell

Plaque - brass: a memorial made of brass

The end of an era page

Protectorate - a state or territory controlled by a more powerful state

Decline - change toward something smaller or lower

Hindrance - the act of hindering or obstructing or impeding

Punitive expedition - the military excursion sent by the British in 1897; which totally destroyed the sophisticated West African kingdom of Benin

Massacre - kill a large number of people indiscriminately

Treaty - written agreement between two states or sovereigns

Appease - make peace with

Atonement - compensation for a wrong

Consul - a representative of a foreign government

Exiled - to be sent away from one's home (city, state or country) while either being explicitly refused permission to return and/or being threatened by prison or death upon return

Loot - plunder: steal goods; take as spoils

Routed - direction diverted

Brain teasers

History quiz:

When and where was the Kingdom of Benin?
Who were the Binis?
Kings of Benin timeline
What was childhood like?
What gods did they worship and why?
What food did they eat?
What food did they eat?
What jobs did the people do?
What goods did they trade and with whom?
Why did the Kingdom of Benin end/ collapse?
What was the scramble for Africa?

Geography quiz:
Where was/ is Benin in the world?
What is the climate in Benin like?
What is the weather like?
What is the population of Benin?
What languages do the people speak?
Does Benin have a monarchy and why?

Further reading

Web links:

http://www.bbc.co.uk/schools/primaryhistory/worldhistory/benin_bronze/

http://beninhistorya.blogspot.co.uk/

http://iyiomon.blogspot.co.uk/

http://www.britishmuseum.org/PDF/british_museum_benin_art.pdf

http://www.conceptvessel.net/iyare/index.html

http://edoworld.net/Obas.html

http://edoworld.net/Benin_bronze.html

http://en.wikipedia.org/wiki/Benin_Empire#Monarchs

http://en.wikipedia.org/wiki/Oba_of_Benin

Printed in Great Britain
by Amazon.co.uk, Ltd.,
Marston Gate.